W9-BYX-897

# Riding
## the Ferry
## with
# Captain
# Cruz

**Written by**
**ALICE K. FLANAGAN**

**Photographs by**
**CHRISTINE OSINSKI**

Reading Consultant
LINDA CORNWELL
Learning Resource Consultant
Indiana Department Of Education

**CHILDREN'S PRESS®** *A Division of Grolier Publishing*
New York • London • Hong Kong • Sydney • Danbury, Connecticut

1

*Special thanks to Daniel Cruz*
*for allowing us to tell his story.*

*Also, thanks to Captain Mauldin and*
*the New York Department of Transportation.*

**Library of Congress Cataloging-in-Publication Data**
Flanagan, Alice.
   Riding the ferry with Captain Cruz / by Alice K. Flanagan; photographs by Christine Osinski.
      p.   cm. — (Our neighborhood)
   Summary: Simple text and photographs describe the duties and responsibilities of Captain Cruz, a ferry boat captain who takes people back and forth from Staten Island to New York City.
   ISBN: 0-516-20046-1 (lib. bdg.)—0-516-26059-6 (pbk.)
   1. Ferries—New York  (State)—Staten Island—Juvenile literature. [1. Ship captains. 2. Occupations. 3. Staten Island Ferry. 4. Ferries.] I. Osinski, Christine, ill. II. Title. III. Series: Our neighborhood (New York, N.Y.)
   VM421.F55  1996
   386'.6'0974726—dc20
                                         96-17145
                                              CIP
                                              AC

Photographs ©: Christine Osinski

Hear the horn blow?
Hurry!
The ferryboat is leaving.

See the captain on deck?
That's Mr. Cruz, my neighbor.

All day long, Captain Cruz takes people back and forth from Staten Island to New York City, across the bay.

Before the ferry leaves,
the crew makes sure everything
on board works.
The trip must be safe!

9

Hear the engines hum?

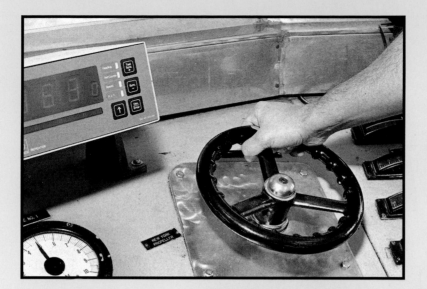

Slowly, Captain Cruz steers the ferry away from the dock.

He checks his compass to see
which direction the ferry is going.

He watches the radar screen.
It shows him how to keep the
ferry on course.

Captain Cruz uses a radio to talk
with his crew.
They are like a family.

A deck hand sits at the captain's
side day and night.
He is an extra pair of eyes
looking out.

Feel the roll of the waves?

The captain handles the ferry well.
He has been a ferryboat captain for
ten years.

He knows all about
the weather and the water currents,

the bridges and the passing ships,

and the famous Statue of Liberty.

Captain Cruz watches these things
each day on his way to and from
the city.

23

Feel the ferry stop?
We have crossed the bay.

After every trip, and at the end of each day, Captain Cruz writes in the captain's log.
He records what happened along the way.

The captain does his job well.

He helps people get to work
safely and on time.

Captain Cruz is careful
and responsible.

With hard work, he has made his dream of being a ferryboat captain come true!

# Meet the Author
# and the Photographer

Alice Flanagan and Christine Osinski are sisters. They grew up together telling stories and drawing pictures in a brown brick bungalow in a southwest-side neighborhood of Chicago, Illinois. Today they write stories and take photographs professionally.

Ms. Flanagan resides in Chicago with her husband and works as a freelance writer. Ms. Osinski is a photographer and teaches at The Cooper Union for the Advancement of Science and Art in New York City. She lives with her husband and two sons on Staten Island.